Dear Frankie

Edited by Patrick O'Dea

MENTOR

This Edition first published 1998 by
MENTOR PRESS
43 Furze Road,
Sandyford Industrial Estate,
Dublin 18

Tel. (01) 295 2112/3   Fax. (01) 295 2114

ISBN: 1 902586 40 9

A catalogue record for this book is available from the British Library

Copyright © Patrick O'Dea 1998

All rights reserved. No part of this publication may be reproduced, stored in a retrieval system, or transmitted in any form or by any means electronic, mechanical, photocopying, recording, or otherwise, without prior written permission of the publisher.

Acknowledgements

The editor and publisher would like to thank the *Irish Press* plc for permission to quote from Frankie Byrne's contributions to the *Evening Press*. The Editor would also like to thank his daughter, Mary O'Dea, aged 11, for her word processing.

Back cover photograph courtesy of RTE Library.

Design and layout: Erin Price

Printed in Ireland by Colourbooks

Contents

Foreword 5

How Are Ya Fixed for Love?
My Sisters, the Flirts 10
My Puritanical Boyfriend.. 12
Glamorous Granny 14
Loosen the Apron Strings 18
TB or Not TB.. 20
It's Essential to Talk – NOW 22
One of You Should Cool It...................................... 24
The Girls of Today 26
No Kiss Yet — Am I a Failure? 28
Office Girls 30

My Way
Live on a Mountainside for Love! 34
Stand By Your Man.. 36
Living Next Door to Mother 38
A Man Needs a Woman, Not a Girl 40
Is My Husband Straying? 42
I Just Want a Night Out with the Lads 44
I'm Embarrassed About Their Set Up 46
A Taste of What I'm Missing 48

Love Me, Love My Mother 50
Waits Hand and Foot on Mother 52

STRANGERS IN THE NIGHT
I'm in Love with a Married Man 56
She's Wary of the Blow-In! 58
Harridan as a Wife 60
Wannabe Slim 62
Modern Living 64
She Should Give Up Her Job 66
Farming in His Blood 68
Holiday Romance Fades like a Suntan 70
I'm Trendy 72
I'm No Snob 74

THE BEST IS YET TO COME
Stand Up and Be Counted 78
Man Eater 80
Rule Book for the Romantic Granny 82
Gyrate with the Best at 36! 84
Was I a Little Hasty? 86
Life Begins at Forty 88
Mummy's Boy 90
I Know I Will Make the Perfect Husband 92
Romance without Explosion 94

FOREWORD

Dear Frankie heralds the passing of an earlier Ireland; of dinners in the middle of the day, of wives in the home. Many of the people associated with Frankie Byrne's radio programme and newspaper column are gone to their reward. The kid from Hoboken, Frank Sinatra, no longer sings the blues. The *Irish Press*, for which Frankie wrote, has ceased to publish.

The rules by which we live have changed and so too has the way we ventilate our distress. Professional listeners now abound. 'Agony Aunts' have become personal columnists and use a language of emotional narrative. For better relationships, *Irish Independent* readers can phone 'On the Couch with Patricia Redlich'. Calls cost 58p per minute. Fans of the *Irish Times* can read 'Living and Loving' by psychologist Maureen Gaffney. Even the internet now provides 'online counselling'. Visit the Counselling Network and use Cyberia's free referral service. Cyberia answers questions like: 'Where did my libido go?' and offers advice on jealousy, commitment, in-laws and eating disorders.

The medium of Irish radio still broadcasts on personal problems, but with a new explicit tone. The tone is that of post-liberal-agenda Ireland, P.C. to the point of parody!

Gay, maybe you think I'm stupid but if there's anyone out there with the same problem as myself I'd love some advice. Philip is a boy but looks like a girl and Rachel is a girl who looks like a boy. With a beard. Then there's Martin, he's a feminine gay, Gay. Oh Gay! Sorry Gay! Anyway Martin's very organised but he does fight sometimes with Seamus the butch gay. And Valerie, God love her, she envies the two of them. She's transsexual. Gillian is next, a butch lesbian who

thinks like a man, I think. Ah, they are, Gay, great kids altogether. All individuals.
('Gender' by Robert English and Carmel Rooney. Performed on *Nighthawks* and the *Gay Byrne Radio Show* by Rosemary Henderson)

Frankie's letters at a stretch might be called 'social history'. But ***Dear Frankie*** is not the full story of relationships in that Ireland. Much remained unspoken.

THE AUTHOR

The public figure Frankie Byrne is best remembered as Ireland's first Agony Aunt. Journalist Michael O'Toole wrote: 'It was impossible to meet her without wanting to open champagne.' She was stylish in the way of Garbo and Dietrich, and spoke in that sort of distinctive voice ideally suited to radio.

Her outstanding achievement was to present *Women's Page*, the Jacob's sponsored radio programme from 1963 to 1985. One thousand radio programmes with, at its peak, one hundred letters per week. The format remained constant; down-to-earth replies to problems of the heart, interspersed with music from Frank Sinatra. These were melodies to match the mood: 'I've got you under my skin', 'I get a kick out of you' and 'My way' to name a few.

Frankie also wrote a 'Dear Frankie' column for Thursday's *Evening Press*, through part of the 1980's. Her piece was located next to 'Petticoat Panel' (sic). Frankie in print expressed the same slightly mocking tone she used on the air. One could hear echoes of her husky voice even on the page of the newspaper.

The more pedestrian side of Frankie's career was the provision to Jacobs of a public relations service. From an early stage, Frankie had worked in PR; first with McConnell's Advertising Agency and later as Frankie Byrne PR Ltd. Prior to her career in PR, Frankie worked for twelve years in the Brazilian consulate in Dublin. Other triumphs Frankie had were her involvement in the foundation of the Jacobs Radio and TV awards and an honourary life membership from the National Union of Journalists.

Frankie hailed from an eminent and fun-loving family of journalists. Her father, 'Sport' Byrne, was a racing correspondent for the *Irish Press*. Two of her brothers followed their father into that career. Of five siblings, tragically three died in their early middle years. Frankie shared her life with Esther, her beloved sister and colleague.

Frankie Byrne died peacefully on 11 December 1993 in St. Vincent's Hospital, Dublin.

— Patrick O'Dea

Patrick O'Dea is a sociology graduate from Trinity College Dublin. He has previously written A Class of Our Own *(1994).*

How Are Ya Fixed for Love?

My Sisters, the Flints

Dear Frankie,
   I'm desperately in need of some advice and you are the one I'm turning to with my problem.

I'm one of a family of five — I have two brothers and two sisters and I am the youngest — I'm 17 (nearly 18) and my two sisters are 19 and 20. I have no trouble about having boyfriends, but the thing is that whenever I bring one home, one of my sisters begins to flirt with him and my boyfriend seems to lose interest in me. I know they're both better looking than me — although I'm considered quite attractive — and I don't know why this should happen because they've lots of boys of their own.

I'm thinking of running away from home but I don't know where to go. Could you give me some address in Dublin where I could stay? I've never been to Dublin so I don't know my way round. Please don't print my name or address.
   Yours sincerely
   Anon

My Sisters, the Flirts

A. The answer to both your requests is a big NO. No, I will not print your name or address and most definitely, NO, I will not give you any addresses in Dublin. Running away is not the answer to your problem or any problem in fact and I strongly advise you to put that idea out of your head this minute.

Your situation is quite common when you happen to be one of Three Lovely Lassies in a family . . . particularly if you're the youngest.

Somebody older — mentally — with superior defence mechanisms would have said that the other two sisters were said to be prettier; only the very young or the very old would admit to being considered less attractive. I'm quite sure you are maybe as attractive as they are, maybe more attractive in some ways, but you just haven't achieved their self-confidence . . . yet.

In a family of three girls one is bound to be better looking than the others — but there are so many different types of beauty how can you possibly place yourself a poor third? You've got the wrong attitude altogether — life isn't a beauty contest you know, we all have something to offer and time takes care of a lot of imaginary problems. You appear to have a fixation about your sisters taking your boyfriends and that's a very dangerous thing because if you allow a fixed idea about anything to take root, all you're doing is placing a padlock on your mind and no argument or even evidence will shake your conviction, because it is not based on reason or fact but on an emotional judgement.

My Puritanical Boyfriend

Dear Frankie,

My boyfriend is a very puritanical man and basically does not like attractive women. He disapproves of make-up, sheer tights, jewellery, tight sweaters and jeans. He's had a number of girlfriends before me, but he gave them up because he said they were too pretty and flamboyant (whatever that means) — at least that's what he's told me.

The truth is that I think he likes me because I'm no beauty — I'm not even very pretty, although I'd have to say he's no oil painting himself, but passable. I'm by no means ugly, but kind of plain, although I have a good figure and I'm told an attractive personality!

The thing is, he wants to marry me. He has a good job and his father has promised him the family home when he marries (his Dad will move out to another smaller house he owns). There's talk of marriage and he's anxious that we'd marry and be settled in by Christmas. He's a good and kind man but I'm not sure I could make myself into the kind of person he wants. What do you think I should do?

Yours sincerely
Plain Jane

My Puritanical Boyfriend

A. Well he certainly has you brainwashed, to make you use such a *nom de plume* and that would be my worry where you're concerned. It's difficult enough to be yourself or what you want to be, but when that means going against your natural impulses, it could become a crippling task and I wouldn't make too many promises before marriage if I were you.

Any connection between your boyfriend's aversion to attractive women and his puritanical convictions is purely coincidental, believe me. If it were wrong to be attractive, or even strive to be attractive, we'd have learned it from the Penny Catechism or whatever religious instruction books you got your basic training from. If you're going to give into him on this score, it won't be long before he'll be adding a few 'thou shalt nots' of his own.

Personally, I think he's just unsure of himself and thinks he can only be safe with someone equally insecure — and it wouldn't be long before you couldn't cross the street without his permission or support. When one partner in a marriage is insecure, it's vitally important that the other half should be strong and confident.

I don't really believe this is an either/or situation. Perhaps your 'attractive' predecessors just wouldn't tolerate this man's attitude and sent him packing. But then again, maybe he's just fundamentally a serious-natured man, who just couldn't cope with the kind of phoney sophistication some girls confuse with maturity. What sort of marriage would you have if both of you turn away completely from the mainstream of life?

I don't say everything about life is perfect, but it's the only life we have and it's our duty to make the best of it, if our limited time on this planet is not to be wasted.

Glamorous Granny

*D*ear Frankie,

I am a widow of 63 (almost 64 I must admit) but I have always been very particular to keep myself as young and active as possible and I probably look younger than I am. Nevertheless, Frankie, that really has nothing to do with my present problem.

My married daughter and family live quite close and we all see a lot of each other — and in fact we always have a weekend lunch at either my house or theirs. She made a very good marriage and I was very pleased with her choice — it's worked out very well and they have two beautiful children whom I adore.

All was well up to about six months ago, when I noticed that her husband — my son-in-law — started paying extra attention to me. At first it was a kind of flattery, then a form of flirting and lately he's started making advances to me — even in front of my daughter. I'm desperately worried about this because I'm just an ordinary gran. I had over 40 years of happy marriage and I'm not at all interested in replacing my husband, as I'm quite happy as I am. I find it all very embarrassing.

On two occasions he dropped over in the evening to see me. Each time he has had some excuse he made up, but I know he just wanted to be with me alone. The first time he arrived alone he said he'd noticed one of the wall plugs needed fixing, and the last time it was to bring me a book I'd mentioned casually a few days before.

My daughter knew he was coming over because in fact she had sent the book — but she doesn't know what I know and that is his overfriendly manner with me. I had thought of mentioning it to her but I'm terrified of a split and I just couldn't bear anything to happen which would stop me seeing my daughter and my adorable grandchildren.

Glamorous Granny

I'm really quite fond of my son-in-law if only he would treat me as his mother-in-law and not as a woman — if you know what I mean. Can you suggest a course of action I could take to put things right so that we could just go on being a happy family?
Yours sincerely
Glamorous Granny

Glamorous Granny

A. I'm trying very hard to find a way to reply to your letter and to put your mind at ease without hurting your feelings and damaging your self-esteem.

You certainly are a mixture of the modern and old-time little old lady. At one point in your letter you refer to yourself as just an 'Ordinary Gran' — you had already stressed that you look much younger than you are and have always been very particular to keep yourself as young and active as possible. All very commendable except I don't know what you mean by an ordinary gran — I shouldn't imagine there's any such person — but then you sign yourself 'Glamorous Granny'.

Now unless you're keeping back something sinister from your letter I will be blunt and honest. You are absolutely misinterpreting your son-in-law's behaviour towards you and I must beg you not to take any course of action whatsoever either with him or your daughter — just don't let your imagination run away with you. There are some women who could be termed ageless — not only in their physical appearance but also in their attitude to life. These are the fortunate ones who are totally unaware of any barriers between generations and who consequently sail through life accepted unquestioningly by the very old and the very young. Somehow or other they just remain more or less the same right through their lives and you are obviously outstanding in this category.

Now you cannot expect to be treated like 'Dear Old Gran' all of a sudden by your daughter or her husband, when up to now they see you as one of them — you three are obviously good friends who enjoy each other's company and who love each other. If your son-in-law happens to have an outgoing generous personality, for heaven's sake don't start reading anything else into his behaviour — this would create such an embarrassing situation that you just never could

Glamorous Granny

restore the same relationship between you all again.

As a safety clause and just in case you are not telling me everything, if his 'advances' progress beyond the flirtatious stage when your daughter is not present, then, of course, you must take a course of action — but I suggest you first of all take one of your friends into your confidence before you drop the bomb by having a family showdown.

Loosen the Apron Strings

D*ear Frankie,*
My son is in his mid-thirties and up to now he hasn't been bothered much with dating girls — in fact he's never really had what is called a 'steady girlfriend'. I'm a widow and he's very devoted to me but while I wouldn't try to put him off girls, he hasn't had any experience and now I'm a bit concerned because of a girl he met on holiday recently.

She is in her twenties — almost thirty — and lives in Edinburgh where she has a very good job. He has shown me photographs and she certainly is a beauty — very much the modern girl — beautifully dressed and I would imagine very sophisticated. This worries me, because my boy is a simple ordinary fellow and I know they write to each other at least once a week because while he doesn't show me the letters, when the post arrives, he gets so elated and calls out to me: 'Here's a letter from . . .' and then he spends hours in his room writing to her. He's very secretive about the situation between them and I'm afraid he'll walk himself into a breach of promise case if he's not careful about what he writes but when I bring up the subject he gets very cross with me.

We lead a quiet life here and I'm sure it wouldn't suit her. How can I get him to see this for himself? She's coming over for a visit soon, but I'm hoping he'll have gone off her by then. How can I do this? It's for his own good.
Yours sincerely
Upset

Loosen the Apron Strings

A. 'For his own good' — how many times have we heard this when someone wants to get their own way? Here we have the classic situation of mother unwilling to untie the apron strings. Some mothers regards their sons — particularly when they're still living at home at the ripe old age of 35 — as simple boys, and the older they become the more simple they appear to their mothers.

Don't fool yourself into thinking that just because he's still single and hasn't bothered much with dating girls (as far as you know) that he doesn't know anything about them. The direct opposite could be true. Maybe his observations if not his experience has led him to give them a miss . . . until now, when according to your letter, he has at last met Ms. Right.

You shouldn't make a judgement until you meet — and even then you should be delighted to see your son so happy. It looks like a serious alliance to me so I suggest you stop working yourself into a fever of suspicion that she might trap your son into writing something he couldn't get out of. What you really mean is something YOU couldn't get out of.

I think in your heart and soul you know that one day your son is going to get married and settle down to a life of his own and I suggest you start preparing yourself for that now. You're still trying to live his life for him and whether it's a girl writing from across the water or a girl meeting him at the crossroad, this is something he'll decide for himself — no matter how you worry. Consider this girl as a human being, anxious for friendship and just probably terrified at the thought of meeting you. Give her a welcome; cut those apron strings — he's a grown man now with his own life to lead.

TB or Not TB

Dear Frankie,
Although I'm originally from the country I've been living in Dublin for years. I have a splendid job as a cook in a hotel and I like it very much, but I'd also like to be married.

I'm 39 and my fellow is 42 — he has a small farm in Co. Galway but he drives up to see me once a week and also when there's a match at Croke Park. He says we'll marry when his herd of cows is free from TB, which could be another two years. Should I wait or chance taking a Dublin man who is always bothering me with marriage proposals in the kitchen? I can't afford to play hard to get at 39.
Yours sincerely
Undecided

TB or Not TB

A. TB or not TB — that is the question. I wonder if this is a long-finger exercise but somehow I don't doubt his intentions and I don't think you do either. It's the fact that you're 39 that's worrying you, isn't it? Well, it shouldn't and if you intend to be a farmer's wife you'd better learn something about the business — its ups and downs — and show concern and understanding about his present problems. Bovine TB is a serious matter and I'm sure he's worried to death.

As for your city slicker, slipping into the kitchen with marriage proposals — while you're slaving over a hot oven. If he's serious why doesn't he bring you out somewhere for a meal and whisper sweet nothings while someone else is doing the cooking? Whether you say yes or no is up to you, but the real crux I think is the fact that you were born in 1946 instead of 1966. Forget about that. Any woman who can command two applicants for her hand in marriage can afford to relax — many a girl half your age isn't as well off as you in the marriage stakes.

It's Essential to Talk — NOW

Dear Frankie,
   I am a man in my mid-thirties and I'm going out with this girl for nearly six years — she's 29. I love her very much and have asked her to marry me. She says she loves me and I believe it. I adore her and we spend all our time together. I've a good job and there are no obstacles — even our families like each other. Yet, she always puts me off, saying she's not ready to settle yet. She never gives me a reason.

   I'd love a home and a family, and after six years I would have thought she'd know her own mind. Any advice or explanation, Frankie?
   Yours sincerely
   Puzzled

It's Essential to Talk — NOW

A. It's very puzzling. If only I knew something more about this girl I'd be better able to help you perhaps. But I think that if only you knew something more about her, you wouldn't have this problem. It's not unusual for a woman — or a man — to be happy with a long-term relationship, yet recoil from making a lifetime commitment. A sort of emotional claustrophobia which could be preventing her from going beyond the point of no return, as she may see it.

On the other hand, if she is inexperienced, she may be apprehensive about the sexual aspect of marriage. If this is the case, it is essential that you discuss this together or attend a pre-marital course. You must have a serious talk with her — now.

One of You Should Cool It

Dear Frankie,

I'm sure you've heard it said that the way to a man's heart is through his stomach. Well, I live in a small town and I've been going out with a farmer's son for about eighteen months. He's friendly with my family and he comes to our house a lot. My mother is a fantastic cook — I'm not bad myself, either. Well, he gets the best of everything here and in spite of all the attention, he's never mentioned marriage yet. I've heard he has been seen in a nearby town with almost every girl in the hall. I'm wondering if I and my mother are doing the right thing by giving him all this good food and attention. What do you think?

Yours sincerely
Carmel

One of You Should Cool It

A. Well I've heard that the way to a man's heart is through his stomach all right, but I never heard it said that it was a short cut. You and your mother are overdoing this. When one woman fusses over a man, he thinks he's lucky — but when two women wait on him hand and foot, he begins to believe that they're the lucky ones. One of you at least should cool it for a while. There's an old saying, 'A comfortable relationship is not conducive to an early marriage.' Think about that for a while and then draw your own conclusions, then perhaps you might draw up a fresh campaign of action — a bit more low key and discreet. Forget about the dance hall — as long as he's dancing with every girl in the place you've nothing to worry about.

The Girls of Today

Dear Frankie,
Quite honestly, I'm very disillusioned with the permissiveness of so many girls today. I'm 28, good-looking, eligible and all too willing to respect the opposite sex if only I got some encouragement. But many of the girls who write to you suggest that we men just prey on innocent girls — which is far from true. After the first date, it's invariably the girl who will phone with some excuse and try to make another date and after a couple of meetings, you're hooked.

While women may like to be pursued, you should tell those girls that not all men like girls who are willing to spend their Saturday nights going from pub to pub and then onto a disco and back to someone's place for a party until daybreak. Now you may well say that a man gets the kind of girl he's looking for, so why am I complaining? Well I'll tell you. Some of us men would like to feel that some things are not to be had simply for the asking . . . and the majority of girls I meet are far too anxious to please us men, if you follow me.

Yours sincerely
Joe

The Girls of Today

A. Well, if I follow you correctly, would I be right if I conclude that here we have superman who would be happier if the girls you fancy were — let's say — not so eager to surrender to your magic charm? I deplore your generalisation and condemnation of the girls who join you and the boys at the weekends. And if what you say is true, why do YOU think it's true? Could it be, thrown as they increasingly are into a man's world, they try to adapt themselves to what they think is a masculine scale of values? I wonder how many girls who have been out with men like you would recognise your self-portrait of 'innocence betrayed'. And if they behave as you say, then how do you think they got that way?

I think it is a bit unfair to adopt such a puritanical attitude towards the girls in your group . . . they all set out to enjoy themselves just like you. And so what if you get a call from one of those girls . . . if you don't want to meet again, you're quite free to make one excuse or another. There's really no hard or fast way about this kind of thing — some men like to take the initiative and some who are too shy to make the first move, would be delighted to get one of those phone calls which seem to ruin your image of women. My advice to you would be to lead your own life according to your standards and don't be afraid that this will ruin your manliness in any way. Personally, I think your going around with the wrong crowd — for you.

No Kiss Yet — Am I a Failure?

Dear Frankie,
Although I'm now 22 — nearly 23 — I've only started to socialise recently. For the past few months, I've been going out with a very nice boy — a student — but there are a few things that I'm a bit concerned about. To begin with, I should tell you that while we meet at least twice or three times a week when we go for a walk or meet some friends in the pub (he doesn't drink by the way) or the cinema, there are evenings when he can borrow his brother's car and we can drive out to a dance. Why am I concerned?

Well, he never pays for my ticket to go into the dance and the other thing is he rarely kisses me goodnight — maybe sometimes a peck on the cheek. You can see he's not very demonstrative! He tells me I look great in jeans but my mother is always telling me to wear a dress going to the dance — anyway that's not very important. What I want to know is am I a failure? . . . because surely after two months together, he'd make some attempt at being a bit more familiar with me. Would it be a good idea if I should try to kiss him on the way home? . . . he is a bit shy but I'm very fond of him.

Yours sincerely
Orla

No Kiss Yet — Am I a Failure?

A. Are you a failure? At 22? . . . and all because your boyfriend hasn't got around to kissing you goodnight after knowing you for two months! You've got a treasure there, but you don't realise it. On no account try to kiss him on the way home . . . let him keep his mind on his driving and his eyes on the road if you want to live to see 23. You don't realise this and you probably won't be grateful for me telling you this — but you are now drawing the dividends for leading a sheltered life until now.

So many girls have been in and out of love — several times — at nineteen and nothing less than a shooting match between them and a jealous rival would create the excitement you're going through now. Years from now, you'll fondly look back and tell yourself 'Those were the golden years' — I can never understand why most of us don't realise it when things are going sweetly for us . . . one of the complexities of life I suppose. The boy is obviously very interested in you but your big worry is that he doesn't pay your way into the dances, nor give you any hassle when you go out on an evening. Only a couple of weeks ago, I was trying to reassure a troubled correspondent that all boys who bring a girl out are not just after the 'one thing', as she termed it — and here you come, miserably disappointed that you don't have to call for help when the boy leaves you home! So he doesn't buy your ticket at the dance hall — so what? This boy is a student, he's not earning money at the moment, and I imagine it takes all his resources to be able to pay for himself — this is and always was the common practice under these circumstances. You're luckier than most. From some of the letters I get, most of the boys don't even arrive with their girlfriends — they 'meet inside'. How would you like that? Stop making trouble for yourself and let things take their course . . . just because he likes you in jeans, don't assume he isn't capable of wearing the pants if you push him too far.

Office Girls

Dear Frankie,

Either last week or the week before, you were replying to a 'young married woman' who felt her husband neglected her and I found it very interesting to know that — although you don't use this expression — you made it very clear that we can be jealous of things as well as people. You're quite right and I wish that was my problem, but I'm just one of millions of women who is just plain jealous of other people! But here's the crunch which makes me a bit unique . . . I am excruciatingly jealous of some people I've never even met!

Can you please write back something that will make me take a pull and stop being so foolish? I'm happily married to . . . yes a young executive . . . who works very hard and is doing well. He discusses his job with me, and he loves his job and the people he works with. We're married five years now and I'm certainly not neglected and his hours are pretty normal. He spends most of his free time with me and the children and I don't resent the fact that his work comes first or if he has to go to the odd night meeting, as he is doing all this for us as well as himself.

But to get to the point, I'm almost out of my mind with jealousy over all those glamorous girls in his office and the sophisticated business women he deals with. He was at home with 'flu' recently and I nearly went out of my mind when I heard him talking to some of those girls on the phone (he had to get in touch now and then) . . . laughing and joking just the way he does with me. And then one evening I was collecting him from the office and he asked me to meet him at the local (office) pub and, once there, all those voices I had spoken to on the phone became a reality.

Office Girls

They were just as I imagined . . . attractive, full of personality and, of course, charming to me, and they were hanging on every word my husband said. There's a whole world out there and I'm not part of it and I can't accept that anyone who shares him all day could resist him. Now one of those girls had an engagement ring on and another had her boyfriend with her but even that didn't stop me from being jealous. I know you're in business yourself and work with a lot of men — married and single — so I thought you'd be interested to hear how a disturbed wife feels.

Yours sincerely
Katie

Office Girls

A. You're right, Katie and I also know how a disturbed husband feels. I never cease to wonder at the remote control some wives seem to exercise over their busy husbands! A number of restless wives are busy creating a myth of their exclusion but believe me, the clever ones are never far from their husbands' minds . . . you're just creating trouble for yourself with this non-existent insecure fantasy of yours.

I'm not diminishing your husband's charms but when a group from the office go off to the local after work with the boss, and knowing his wife is coming in to visit him, it's a wise girl indeed who hangs on his every word and laughs at his jokes in the mistaken belief that you'd be delighted to see what a great guy your husband is and how popular he is at work. And why shouldn't they be beautifully dressed and full of charm?

There is life after 5pm, you know . . . and they were all off somewhere too with other attractive men. But you're right, your husband's working day is a different world but he obviously knows how to make the best of both his worlds. His colleagues and friends work hard to make him feel secure and happy so that he can breeze home and make you feel secure and happy. You can be sure if you had any grounds for jealousy, the office local is the last place he'd suggest for a meeting with his wife.

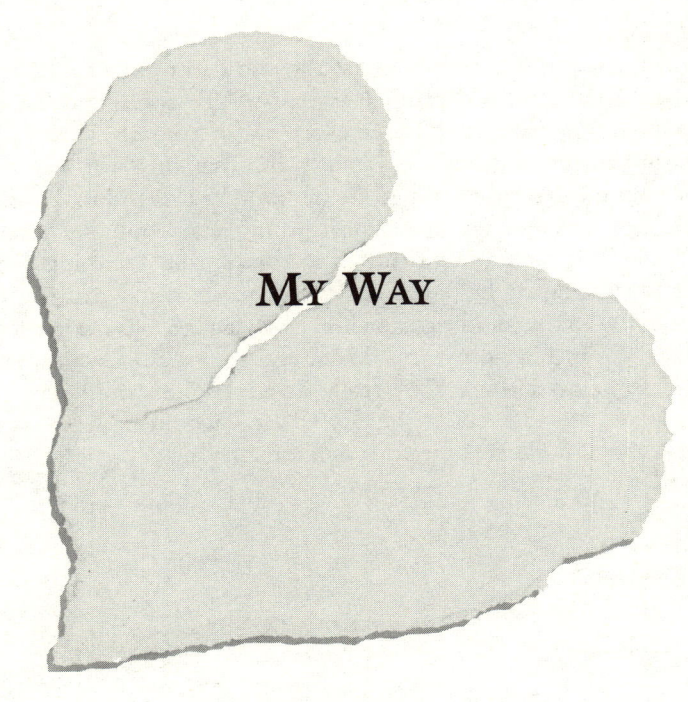

Live on a Mountainside for Love!

D*ear Frankie,*

I'm a country girl, now living in Dublin and I love the city. I have a good job, a very nice boyfriend and we had planned to marry fairly soon. Suddenly everything is in a mess . . . he has inherited a good farm and a house from his uncle and he's thrilled. Well I'm not thrilled, even though he assures me that his farm and house are very modern and I wouldn't have the kind of life my mother had to live — one of drudgery and hard work with no amenities and almost primitive surroundings, miles away from anywhere. I should have mentioned that he too comes from a farming background, but unlike me, he always hoped he'd get back to that life some day. This farm he has inherited is not in fact in the middle of nowhere — in fact he tells me it is less than twenty miles from a very flourishing provincial town, and we would have quite a lot of near neighbours. Nevertheless I think if he really loved me he would stay in Dublin and maybe sell this property, and stay in the city where I would be happy. I'm sure you'd agree with me — but I'd like to hear your opinion anyway.

Yours sincerely
Country Girl

Live on a Mountainside for Love!

A. So you think this born and bred farmer should stay in the city where you would be happy? Now why would any sensible man throw away a chance of a lifetime to do something with his life which he's always hoped for, just to please a stubborn young girl who apparently thinks she's a better person than her mother was? Your mother must have been a good, resourceful, uncomplaining woman but don't fool yourself that her hard working life is frightening you off. Her hard times bear no relation to the home comforts this young man is offering you and you know that perfectly well.

Basically what it comes down to is this. You want to live in Dublin, he wants to grab the good fortune that comes his way and go back to the life he knows and loves. If you love him, you'd live on a mountainside with him, but if you blackmail him into your way of thinking, you may never know a day's happiness. It's a choice between suburban comfort or rural comfort and if it's too big a risk for you, then pick up your marbles and get out of the game.

Stand By Your Man

Dear Frankie,
My husband and I had a business of our own — it ran into financial difficulties and we had to sell our home to meet his debts. I wasn't in great health at the time and I really needed my husband, but he was working all the time even at weekends, although he must have known in his heart the situation was hopeless.

I wanted to share his worries — to help him — but he just shut me out and wouldn't even discuss it with me in the evenings. When we had to sell the house, I thought he would need me for comfort but he just ignored me. Now, I feel a total failure as a woman. As long as I get his meals and look after our small flat — that seems to be all I'm good for. He just watches television every night and seems to be content but I feel so frustrated and invisible with my misery. I start shouting at him just to make him notice me and then I feel ashamed afterwards. I think he's very selfish but he's so placid and is behaving as if I didn't exist. What should I do to make him notice me again?

Yours sincerely
Ignored

Stand By Your Man

A. You can take it that he has noticed you all right and from your account of your behaviour in a time of crisis I'd say you're a lucky woman to be in one piece. So you feel a failure as a woman? How do you think he feels as a businessman who has — like so many businessmen today — lost out to the economic depression and has to see his life's work disappear before his eyes? Your husband hasn't only lost his business but his pride, I presume. And there you are, like a spoiled child, screaming for attention. I'm being a bit hard on you, perhaps, but at a time like this you really should be more understanding and sympathetic. Now is the time he needs your support — not your aggression.

Living Next Door to Mother

Dear Frankie,
I'm engaged to be married to a man I love very much and he feels the same about me, but now coming up to our wedding date — the end of June — we're not seeing eye to eye on a very important issue. It's all about where we're going to live. I had been looking forward to a house of our own — my fiancé has a well-paid job and I'm working, but now his mother has put this proposition to us . . . as a kind of wedding present. She has a lovely house — no one else lives there except my boyfriend. A few years ago she had a bungalow built in the garden — beautifully furnished, three bedrooms, central heating — in fact all mod cons. She has it let but the tenant's lease is up next month and my future mother-in-law has offered this bungalow to us rent-free as a gift.

John is thrilled but I don't want to move in with anyone — I was looking forward to having our own home. Much as I like my future mother-in-law, and even though it has a separate entrance and, of course, our own front door, I feel she would be on top of us all the time. Would I be right to hold out for what I want or am I being selfish? John has good prospects for promotion and we could do better.

Yours sincerely
Undecided

Living Next Door to Mother

A. John may have good prospects for promotion, but bear in mind the way things are going now, he also has good prospects for redundancy.

I don't wish to depress you but really you should be a bit more practical about this problem. Are you being selfish, you ask? I think you could be described as being foolish. I appreciate your longing for the home of your dreams, but have you thought about what it's like to have a long-term mortgage hanging over your head for years? Lots of couples do this of course, but I doubt if they have an alternative as attractive as yours.

You're not moving in with your mother-in-law you know. Here you have a ready-made home, fully furnished, free gratis and for nothing. Everything here seems so advantageous and attractive, I find myself thinking again about this view of marriage as a blueprint for a whole new life and your letter spells it out. Here you are with a wealthy generous mother-in-law, apparently devoted to you, who wants to present you with a beautiful home where you can be together — but separate. It's not bad when you think of all the couples who have to endure hostile landlords and landladies and pay them handsomely to live in their homes with far less comfort than I'm sure you'll have.

You are not going to live under the same roof, you are just going to be neighbours, and as the years go by you and John can keep an eye on her and you will inherit a built-in babysitter. What more can you want? If the Ewings can do it in Southfork, why can't you?

A Man Needs a Woman, Not a Girl

Dear Frankie,
I was married when I was 18, that was 17 years ago, and we have twins of 16. They are our only children. My husband treats me very badly and has done so for years in fact. Now he's not violent physically, but he seems to have no regard for me whatever.

He has been unfaithful to me on a number of occasions and at the moment he's having an affair with a woman I know to see quite well — but, of course I have never spoken to her about it. I have spoken to my husband and threatened to leave. He says I can go if I want to, but I don't think I could manage alone and I don't want to leave the children or do anything that might upset them. I don't think they are aware of the situation as we don't have shouting rows — but when I asked my husband why he married me, he said it seemed like a good idea at the time. I would be hopeless on my own but I feel that he should have some regard for me, even out of duty.

What sort of woman would have an affair with a married man? She ought to be ashamed of herself. My husband says I'm like a child — and I've tried to get him to talk it out with me, but he won't even sit down to listen. Do you think he'll ever change or should I leave him?

Yours sincerely
Lydia

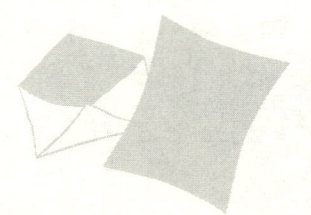

A Man Needs a Woman, Not a Girl

A. You've answered the last question yourself — and from your letter I've got to agree with you. I just don't think you could manage on your own, not in your present state of mind anyway. And as for his changing, I just don't know what to say. I think if YOU changed, there is a chance he might start acting differently. Now why does he say you are like a child — and why have you allowed your marriage to get to this stage?

If he won't sit down and talk to you, I suppose it's useless to mention a marriage counselling service. Now you must have had something good together in the early days. Could you cast your mind back and see where things went wrong? — and don't make the mistake of exempting yourself from some of the blame. This domination and contempt from your husband couldn't have happened overnight, so perhaps you haven't asserted yourself sufficiently.

You know a man wants and needs a woman in his life — not an ageing dependent girl. So ask yourself, have you matured since your wedding day? Have you a personality of your own, friends of your own, interests of your own? In fact do you exist at all except as an appendage of your husband's life and mother of his children? Wife and motherhood are all important — but your husband obviously needs more.

Your children are now at an age where they no longer require your fulltime attention, so would you consider taking some part-time job, if you can get it, or some voluntary commitments as you obviously can afford the time and, I suspect, the money.

Is My Husband Straying?

D*ear Frankie,*
 I've been married for almost two years and as far as I am aware — happily married. But for the past six months or so, I've had a feeling that my husband is seeing another girl. I can't exactly put my finger on it, but some of the warmth between us seems to have gone. One thing that has me suspicious is the fact that whenever I go out in the evenings, he always asks me what time I'll be back at, and he never used to do that before. Also he seems a lot more casual in his day-to-day behaviour to me and he doesn't seem to talk as much as he did at the beginning. There are times when his thoughts seem to be miles away.

Well I swore I couldn't bring up the subject with him, but I did — more than once — and he nearly went off the deep end, and asked me was I losing my mind. I wish I could believe him and trust him as I did in the beginning, but so many small things he says or does make me suspicious. Can you give me any advice to give me back my peace of mind? I'm absolutely miserable at the moment.

Yours sincerely
Mary

Is My Husband Straying?

A. Well, I wouldn't say you are the only one who is miserable at the moment. Your husband must be going through hell from your jealousy and suspicion. What on earth has got into you? I most certainly do not suspect your husband on the basis of the evidence you've put forward. Do you honestly believe if he is having an affair, he would choose his own home as his love nest? If that's all you have to go on, then forget it. You might have something to worry about if he started disappearing every evening and coming home in the early hours after a night out with the lads, or some heavy overtime in the office. Even then you should be more trusting until you had positive proof he was going off the straight and narrow.

Tell me, have you asked yourself why you've begun to behave like this? Is there any area in your life or in your relationship that makes you feel you deserve to be betrayed by your husband? If there is, you do need help and assurance and you should discuss this openly with your husband or with your doctor, because before you believe him and trust him, you must believe and trust yourself. And until you trust him you're never going to have a happy marriage — so do something now, before you drive him away.

I Just Want a Night Out with the Lads

D*ear Frankie,*
   I'm 26 and I've been going with the same girl for over two years. We're very much in love and I would like to get engaged and start making plans for marriage. But one thing is holding me back.

Being very much in love, we spend nearly all our time together. But now and then I like to go to a rugby match or over to the internationals with my male friends. There are other occasions where I have to go to business meetings or if I'm working late I might join my workmates in the local — not often — but I would like to feel free now and then.

The thing is, if there is anything I want to do or anywhere I want to go without her, she gets into an awful state and then the row begins. The rows aren't very serious. In fact, I try to make light of it and laugh her out of her sulks, but she says she can't bear to have me out of her sight. I simply don't know how to handle it and of course that's why I'm hesitating about a marriage discussion. Have you any sort of advice at all or even a few comments, Frankie?

Yours sincerely
Joe Soap

I Just Want a Night Out with the Lads

A. Well Joe Soap, you have my deepest sympathy in your present predicament, although you could be a lot worse off — you could be already married to this girl.

'Togetherness' is a fairly recent addition to our vocabulary and one, I think, which has caused a lot of damage to some relationships. Togetherness is great when each half of the couple feels the same about it, but how stifling and suffocating it can become if it gets to the stage of a complete take-over of another human being. I'm aware also of how often insecurity is put forward as an explanation of what, sometimes, are really basically unlikeable characteristics and I'm afraid your girlfriend has a very jealous, suspicious and possessive nature.

Now these traits are very difficult to cure and while you were quite right to try and laugh her out of it at the beginning, it's obvious you have now reached a point of desperation. The time has come to have a serious talk with her about her irrational behaviour and make her see that this is a serious barrier against any possibility of having a life together.

You must start as you mean to go on, and quite frankly, if you don't see any improvement in your relationship then you will have to have a talk with yourself and seriously consider the possibility of whether or not she is the right girl for you.

I'm Embarrassed About Their Set Up

Dear Frankie,
I am a happily married woman in my early fifties with a 23-year-old son in Australia and a daughter of 27 who lives here in Ireland. Frankie, I am writing to you about my daughter as I foresee an awkward situation looming and I'm not sure how to handle it. In the town where she works she met a man six years ago and they fell in love. The relationship became serious and they have been living together since then. Now they have a baby son, six months old, and the three of them are coming home to spend Christmas with us.

I met the 'man in her life' only once — at the christening, in fact — and he seemed to be very fond of my daughter. But somehow or other I wasn't entirely happy about him — he's very self-assured and arrogant and wasn't a bit embarrassed about the set up.

I've never reproached her about not being married — in fact we avoided the subject, but the thing is that there is no reason why they don't marry, no obstacles at all. He has a good job and my daughter has a part-time job so they're quite all right financially. My husband is a very easy going man and he says it's their life and everything will turn out for the best in the end. Of course the baby is adorable and my daughter is very happy, but her boyfriend is so conceited, I can't see what she sees in him.

How should I cope with him while they're here? I have to remember that he might well turn her against us if I bring up any contentious subject and I don't want that to happen. Did you ever find yourself in a situation where you're looking forward like mad to something and at the same time dreading it? A little guidance would be appreciated.

Yours sincerely
Anon

I'm Embarrassed About Their Set Up

A. Like it or not, your husband is right in this case. It is their life and they are making a decision on a very personal matter. Also, there is a reason for them not marrying — very simply, they don't want to get married and as you and your daughter never discussed the situation you've no way of knowing why.

As for your assessment of this man, I would have to say that on the basis of one meeting — and a very emotional occasion at that — you are really not in a position to judge him. But come Christmas, when you're all living under the same roof, you may find your initial reaction was quite wrong. Don't forget he is a human being too, and he must have been very apprehensive and nervous at the thought of meeting you and your husband for the first time. I would imagine that arrogance and conceit you felt was just a façade to cover up his real feelings. So if I were you I'd put aside your first impressions.

How to cope with him at Christmas, you ask. Well, you have been very civilised and sensible so far, so why change? The most important thing is to keep the friendship and trust of your daughter and make sure never to break the family ties. Your support is essential to your daughter — and you must try and see him through her eyes and leave the future to destiny and fate. Whether they are married or not, this man is part of your family. Who knows what will happen in the future? But right now, he is your daughter's chosen partner and the father of your grandson.

A Taste of What I'm Missing

Dear Frankie,
I am 50-plus, a qualified nurse and have two grown children. My husband is a cold, selfish introverted man, entirely wrapped up in his own interests and his work and we haven't had a good family life for years, although I must say he does provide all the material necessary for life and I couldn't fault him there. However we have grown apart — I've accepted this — and have successfully developed my own life because I have lots of vitality and zest for living and I also have great relationships with my children and their friends.

Recently I met a man about my own age and had a brief affair — brief because, of course, he was also married, but his home life was quite different to mine. Because of his commitments, we broke it off with mutual consent, but I've got to say it gave me a taste of what I was missing and I've been desperately unhappy since.

I suppose this pain will pass, but perhaps it would have been better if I hadn't had this bitter-sweet experience. Can life ever be the same again?
Yours sincerely
Anon

A Taste of What I'm Missing

A. The direct answer to your question is No. Life will never be the same again, but do you really want it to be? If you had wanted your life to remain the same you probably wouldn't have embarked on that brief love affair which has changed it.

I think it has served a purpose, and I suggest you look for ways to change your life even more radically now — while you still have your energy and your remarkable ability to function without self-pity. Your children are grown up, your husband doesn't appear to need you or anyone — that's his loss — so the time has come when you must think about what you want for yourself. At least you've discovered that romance and pleasure — brief though it was — brought you to life for a time. Don't be so despairing, you've no reason to believe it won't happen again.

Love Me, Love My Mother

Dear Frankie,

I'm engaged to a wonderful man — kind, thoughtful and generous. We're very much in love and he wants to get married. We have our eye on a very nice house and we'll have to make up our minds about this soon. As I'm writing to you, it all seems ideal except for one flaw . . . his mother.

My fiancé is the younger of two brothers, both doted on by their mother who is a widow and, of course, she's crazy about them. The older brother is married to a very nice girl who has become a great friend of mine. She warned me that when she became engaged, she was nearly driven mad by his mother who tried to tell them what kind of house to buy, where to go on their honeymoon and insisted on them taking her out to a meal or cinema at least once a week.

Well, she put her foot down and had it out with her fiancé. I must say she's a tough cookie and had no intention of playing second fiddle to her future mother-in-law so they came to respect and accept each other and now get on very well together.

My fiancé is very soft where his mother is concerned and wants me to visit her regularly to become good friends. I know this is going to be a bone of contention and I'm wondering if I'll be able to come to terms with this female monster and am I wise to go ahead with the marriage?

Yours sincerely
In Two Minds

Love Me, Love My Mother

A. This is the first of many situations — real or imaginary — you'll have to face when you change your name, and it won't be the worst. In fact, I don't see that you have any problem, but I'm wondering have you any heart or understanding of other people?

This woman, your future mother-in-law, is a human being, perhaps a little over anxious to be helpful, but she could well become your best friend and ally in years to come. If your boyfriend is a kind and gentle person, 'he didn't lick it off the briars', to use an old saying. I know you would like to believe he was created especially for you, but remember most of his good qualities have been inherited from his mother — this 'female monster' as you rudely described her. Do you think your boyfriend and his brother could feel so caring and solicitous about their mother if she didn't have the capacity to love? Could it be that you don't want to accept the fact that anyone else has the right to love him or be loved by him, except you?

Before you've even bought the house, you're beginning to exhibit the same feelings that you see in her. Almost every bride is likely to be a mother-in-law herself some day and as a wife and mother, you'll have to spend a lot of time putting yourself in somebody else's place. Why not start with your new mother-in-law, who is now bracing herself to get on well with that other 'female monster' — her new daughter-in-law.

Waits Hand and Foot on Mother

Dear Frankie,
   I have a family problem, not our family, but my husband's parents. I find it difficult to describe them because I get into such a fury just to think of them and the trouble they are causing us, that I'm almost afraid of what I'll say. So because I want to write to you about this, I'll try to control myself and put down the facts as I see them with no exaggerations so that you get a fair picture of how things are.

We're happily married over eight years now . . . very happily, I'm delighted to say. We have three lovely children and a very nice home. Fortunately he has a good job— we're by no means well off financially, but enough to protect us against debts and we are able to have the children all at school and we don't go mad spending. My husband is great about the house and can turn his hand to anything. He likes to spend most of the time at home in the evenings, but we nearly always go out together for a drink with our friends on a Saturday night. Now, Frankie that's the height of our debauchery— as my mother-in-law might call it.

So what's the problem you're asking? Well, apart from a married sister who also lives in Dublin, my husband is the only member of his family who hasn't emigrated. So he feels a strong sense of loyalty and obligation to his parents, who absolutely take advantage of him . . . particularly his mother who, to put it mildly, can only be described as a tyrant. She expects him to wait hand and foot on them . . . and if a week goes by without him calling to see them, there's murder. As well as that, she will phone up about a leaking roof, a dripping pipe, a broken something and expect him to drop everything at home and drive over to their house, which is right across the city.

Waits Hand and Foot on Mother

He has always jumped into action, but at the moment we're decorating our own house and he has had to make excuses once or twice. Then out come the old chestnuts from his dear mother: 'We don't count anymore . . . just because you have a family of your own, you've no time for us . . . how can you be so ungrateful after all we've done for you all your life . . . your own family is more important than your mother and father who slaved all those years to bring you up' . . . and more of the same.

All of this is having a terrible effect on my husband, because he feels torn between us and guilty about his parents. Needless to say it's not doing our marriage any good. I feel sorry and I try not to add fuel to the fire and in fact we've talked it over. My husband is suggesting that we make a clean break with his parents, so that we can go on living our life. What do you think, Frankie? Incidentally his parents are by no means old and decrepit — they have a lot of friends and are very active, but they never wanted him to get married, not necessarily to me, but to anybody. Please say something.

Yours sincerely
Anon

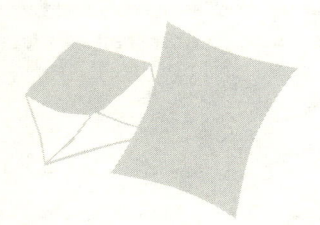

Waits Hand and Foot on Mother

A. Well of course, I'll say something, but your situation needs a lot more than just words, and I'm afraid I'll have to start by being negative. On no account make a break, dirty or clean, with your in-laws. Not entirely for their sake, but if you did that, neither you nor your husband would have an easy moment and it could eventually be totally destructive to your own family's happiness. Try and imagine the remorse if anything were to happen to them — you'd both be haunted mentally for the rest of your lives and as your children get older you would have to bear the burden of their accusations that you deprived them of their grandparents . . . and I don't have to tell you that this is a pretty strong relationship in most family units.

I'm afraid the time has come for you to take over. If your husband has always been so amenable and helpful to his parents, he couldn't possibly handle this situation on his own, but I think you should have a serious talk with his mother, just the two of you. Old habits die hard and she may not even be aware that any situation exists — not if she's always got her own way. To her, your husband is her son — the boy around the house always ready and willing to wait on her hand and foot, as you put it. Well, you better tell her the facts of life, in the nicest, friendliest way possible!

Do not shut them out of your lives, but at the same time don't leave it all to your husband. He can still be willing to help, but not at the expense of his own family. You know, he must be an extraordinarily nice man and you simply can't allow or encourage him to go against his nature without suffering a lot of damage or pain.

Strangers in the Night

I'm in Love with a Married Man

Dear Frankie,
I am in a desperate situation and I am in great need of some guidance, but I feel I can't talk it over with any of my friends. I am in love with a married man for almost two years now, after ten years of complete faithfulness to my husband, in spite of the fact that I have had very little emotional or sexual happiness in all that time. I have two children to whom I am devoted and this man has three children and he dotes on them, but his relationship with his wife is non-existent. He has been quite open with me about his past . . . he has had more than one extra-marital affair during his twelve-year marriage. Although his wife is unaware of all this, we are both now very much in love. He says his responsibilities to his children must keep him tied for the present and I understand that and would wait for him while my children grow up.

What can I do? Do you think I am wasting my time continuing to love him? Should I wait in the wings for some unlikely stroke of fate which would enable us to be together? I am so unhappy . . . as I want us to be together all the time.
Yours sincerely
Unhappy Wife

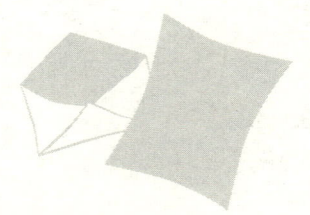

I'm in Love with a Married Man

A. What can I say? There are some questions, you know, that only time can answer, but nevertheless I must admit a chill ran up and down my spine when I got to the part where you might wait in the wings in the event of a 'stroke of fate' which would enable the two of you to be together. It's obvious you are not thinking straight or seeing clearly what sort of a man this is. I am sure he is irresistible to you, but the main thing that would worry me, if I were you, is the fact that he has been chronically unfaithful to his wife since the early years of his marriage. What makes you think you are more special to him than any one of his former lovers who no doubt got the same line of talk as you're getting now?

He sounds to me like the eternal youth who balances out domestic responsibility with extra-marital romps, but in the end always opts for home because that's where he keeps his pipe and slippers. Are you wasting your time in loving him, you ask. Well if you want anything more than love, then 'yes' you are wasting your time.

In your case, I think you want this man as an escape route out of your own wretched marriage and in my opinion, you haven't a hope with him. What about your own two young children to whom you are devoted? Have you given any thought to their future? You can take it that it is most unlikely this man is going to break up his home for you — he's already told you that — so get your priorities right and stop being so self-indulgent. You are wasting your time with him.

She's Wary of the Blow-In!

Dear Frankie,

I am a 38-year-old bachelor — and a very eligible bachelor if I say so myself. I have a well-paid secure job and recently I was transferred from Dublin to a large town in the West of Ireland. When I say recently it was over a year and a half ago, so I regard this place as my own hometown and by now, I know practically everyone here and I love the place. I hope I'll be left here forever . . . it's a great life.

You may wonder why I never married — well I had a few 'entanglements' while I was living in my native Dublin, but I was so dedicated to my career — doing post-graduate degrees and specialised courses and things, that I didn't really have enough time to devote to any one girl. But now Frankie, Cupid has shot his arrow into my heart and I am really in love. The girl I love is a bit younger than I am — about 32 or so. She's from here and I know her family, but that's where the trouble starts. For some reason or other, her mother is not very helpful and while I think she likes me all right, she's not in favour of our getting married.

Now I even have my own house here — I bought it outright before I met this girl — so we've no other problems. How can I get her mother to come round to our way of thinking? What do you think would be the right way of handling this situation without a family break?

Yours sincerely
Eligible Bachelor

She's Wary of the Blow-In!

A. Well, in case you've recently arrived from outer space, let me tell you there is nothing at all unusual about a prospective mother-in-law making difficulties in a case like this, especially when the man concerned arrives like a bolt from the blue into a town where everyone — or almost everyone — knows everyone else. You may be there for the past 18 months, but to some you're still a 'blow-in' — someone to be wary of. But reluctance on the part of a mother in cases like yours is a good sign. It shows she has a good daughter, one that she isn't at all anxious to farm off on a man she doesn't really know yet.

And I think she's a wise one too.

No matter what way things turn out in the future . . . if you end up cursing the unfortunate day you ever clapped an eye on this girl, it can never be said that she was foisted on you by her mother who was anxious to make a good match for her daughter.

If you haven't the gumption at your age to wear down the opposition, you don't deserve this girl . . . so get cracking and direct your charm towards mum. The next time you call to collect 'Juliet', arrive bearing rich gifts for the mother. Some flowers perhaps, although they are not very original. I think a drop of whatever she fancies might be better — Christmas spirit and all that — whatever might coax a happy smile to her face. I can't believe it, a man of 38 afraid of his girlfriend's mother. I'm surprised you don't want me to come down to make the match for you.

Harridan as a Wife

Dear Frankie,
   I'm absolutely miserable and I don't know what to do. For the past six months I have been having an affair with a married man and we've been seeing each other constantly. I don't think he's ever been unfaithful to his wife before — at least he told me I was the first girl he ever looked at since he got married ten years ago. He has three children whom he adores, but according to him his wife is a harridan — unloving, bad-tempered and there's nothing but rows at home.

   I've never met or ever seen his wife, but I do know some of his friends and although they're embarrassed when I ask about her, I've got to admit none of them said a bad word about her. He would be furious if he knew I discussed him with them. Yet about two months ago, he broke it off with me because he said it wasn't fair on his family to be so deceitful.

   Anyway, I accepted it and didn't make a fuss and tried to get on with my life. I had picked up the threads when about two weeks ago, he contacted me again and I just couldn't say no to him. Well it's happened again, Frankie — the same old story: 'We must part, it's not right . . . we love each other but we can't be together' and all the usual platitudes. I said goodbye, but now one of his friends (a very nice man) told me that he had told him and all his pals about us. I feel so embarrassed and so cheap. But will I be able to resist him if and when he contacts me again?
   Yours sincerely
   Miserable

Harridan as a Wife

A. The question is will you be able to resist breaking his neck the next time, if and when you meet? He has been watching too many old movies — that scene is straight out of *Casablanca*, but he'll never be able to hold a candle to the late great Bogie. I am very sympathetic where you are concerned — not because he's a married man — in fact that's the only good part of this whole experience. To think that you might have met him years ago and today you would be playing the role of the deceived wife while he indulged his fancies — preying on gullible young girls like yourself. And the greatest crime of all, recounting his conquests to his buddies. You should be grateful to that pal of his. I would hope this has put you off him forever. Pick up the pieces and get on with your life. He'll be good material when you come to write your memoirs.

Wannabe Slim

Dear Frankie,
   I'm miserable. I am only 19 and have the most terrible weight problem. My height is 5' 3" and I'm nearly eleven stone. Isn't that dreadful, Frankie? Now I work in an office — it's my first job and I was very lucky to get it — and while the people I work with couldn't be nicer, I know they talk about me behind my back and this troubles me a lot. Also I simply would adore to be able to wear the kind of clothes — jeans and things — that my friends wear but I have to keep to sort of 'cover-up' dowdy over-blouses and full skirts.

   What can I do? Don't tell me to diet because I tried a million times and I just can't — I love sweet things and I can't resist them. Please help.
   Yours sincerely
   Jodee

Wannabe Slim

A. To parody a well-known song 'You picked a fine time to diet, Jodee'. Christmas and diets don't go together and I hope you will note that I am ignoring your plea not to tell you to diet. If you want to lose weight, there is no such word as 'can't', and only diet and exercise will do the trick. Diet is really the wrong word. The fact is you must start eating the right foods and give up the fattening foods and you never need to feel hungry.

Your health is at risk. I'm sure you've been told that thousands of times. Eleven stone at your age and height is positively asking for trouble . . . as well as making you feel miserable.

No one is ever really satisfied with their weight. A friend of mine — a slim, lovely girl with a beautiful figure — is convinced she has a 'weight problem'. But according to her husband it's not a weight problem she has, it's a 'food problem'. And yes, she like many of us, has to watch her eating habits.

It's not going to be easy for you. But apart from your health, losing weight will certainly help your self-confidence, which seems to be at a low ebb right now, and rid you of this absurd idea that everyone is talking about you behind your back. Of course they're not. I would imagine the only person who is criticising you is yourself — and if you don't like yourself you're going to find it very difficult to enjoy life. Don't starve yourself at the beginning. Just settle for a gradual reduction and try to walk at least two to three miles a day — half an hour at a time would do. Don't overdo it at the start.

Modern Living

Dear Frankie,
I'm 19 — my boyfriend's 21 — and we've been going together for over three years. Now we've moved into a flat together, but we have a problem. We're not using any form of contraception because he won't use a condom and I won't go on the Pill because I'm afraid of losing my figure. Any advice?
Yours sincerely
Angeline

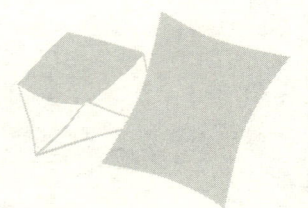

Modern Living

A. If you think the Pill will ruin your figure, just wait and see what pregnancy does to it! On a serious note, however, I sympathise with you and agree that you should not allow yourself to be persuaded to use any form of contraception you dislike . . . whatever your reason.

There are many other forms of contraceptives, most of them extremely efficient, and now that you've set up housekeeping with your boyfriend, I suggest you have a chat with your doctor if you can, or run — do not walk — to your nearest family planning clinic.

She Should Give Up Her Job

D*ear Frankie,*
My 25-year-old son got married recently and both my husband and I were both very pleased with his choice and get on really well with her. She's a year younger than he is. They have a nice house, but I wouldn't say an awful lot of money to throw around. He has a good job and is due for promotion very soon. He is a clever young man and very serious about his work. Outside that he's great fun and he and my daughter-in-law are mad about each other.

Here's the problem, Frankie. I just don't understand some of the young people of today. You see, my daughter-in-law has kept on her own job which entails a good deal of travel during the week so that really they only have the weekends together. If she's lucky, she might only have to be away three days a week and surely that's no way to start married life?

I know they discussed this before the wedding, but I didn't realise her travelling would be a regular thing and I'm desperately worried their marriage won't last, if they're apart so much. I was thinking of having a talk with my son and getting him to ask her to give up her job so that she's home more often. Don't you agree with me, Frankie?

Yours sincerely
Worried Mum

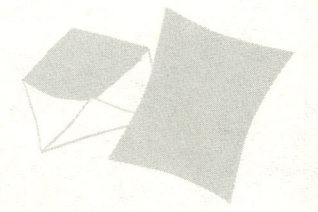

She Should Give Up Her Job

A. The short answer is a very definite 'No, I don't agree with you', but you sound like a well-meaning and caring person so I don't want to be so abrupt with you. In today's wide range of marriage styles, I don't think their arrangement is at all eccentric or risky. It probably seems so to you because more than likely your own marriage was a pretty conventional one, where the husband goes out and makes the money and the wife makes the home and stays in it.

Yes, life has changed since the fifties and even the sixties and you simply must not apply your own attitudes to the present unless you are personally involved in a situation where you must make a decision. Tell me this, if your son's job entailed a lot of travelling and meant his wife was alone for a few days a week, would you feel the same anxiety? Just remember, they are free to make their own decisions and to choose what suits them.

Don't worry about their marriage not lasting and, above all, I would suggest you don't dream of interfering on this point — he's a big boy now and you can be sure he knows what he's doing.

Farming in His Blood

Dear Frankie,

I'm 25 and I've been going with the same boy for the past five years. He wants us to get married and I'm very much in love with him, but there are complications. He lives very near us with his parents and works the family farm with his father — and eventually his brother will join them. It's a very big holding with a 'granny house' which is earmarked for us on the farm, but far enough away from his parents' home not to interfere with us — if and when we marry. He's mad about farming since he was a boy, and always after school helped his father and the farmhands, and then went to an agricultural college.

Now for the snag. My father died a few years ago and he and my mother ran a thriving grocery business together for as long as I can remember. My mother always hoped that when I married, my husband would join our business and run it again as a family concern. Needless to say I discussed this with my boyfriend, but as I guessed, there would be no question of him doing that. I have two sisters, younger than I am. I have discussed my future with my mother and she was so disappointed about her plans about my boyfriend coming into the business falling through, that I was thinking of breaking it off with him. But I know he's the one for me and I couldn't bear to lose him. Can you give me an opinion. I don't know what to do.

Yours sincerely
Confused

Farming in His Blood

A. I think you do know what to do, but it's unfortunate that you can't please everyone in this situation. One thing is certain. Your boyfriend will not be joining your family grocery business. A farmer he is and a farmer he is going to remain. You know yourself that farming is in his blood. It's not an easy life he's choosing, but it's his vocation and in a million years you shouldn't expect him to give it up. I appreciate your mother's disappointment, but while you discussed this with your future husband, I think it's about time the two of you sat down and talked to your mother — and she will see sense.

If you choose to leave this man and hold on until you meet a 'suitable' man who will join your family business, you may well end up in a loveless marriage, and hating your mother. I doubt if you would want that to happen, and I doubt if she would want it either.

It's obvious your mother is a strong personality, a successful business woman, used to having her own way, because your attitude strikes me as strangely cautious in one so young. You must not let your father's death determine your future relationship with any man. Maybe you should ask yourself if your mother's vulnerability in her widowhood might be colouring your present indecision.

It's up to you now. Do something important for yourself — by yourself — by establishing the fact that you are an adult with the right to make your own adult decisions. Your mother hasn't lost out completely. What about your two younger sisters? One of them may well come up with a suitable candidate, so don't feel bad.

Holiday Romance Fades like a Suntan

Dear Frankie,

Recently I went away on a package tour to Majorca and had a fabulous time. I went with two girlfriends and the very first evening we went dancing, would you believe it, I met a terrific boy from my own home town! Now I didn't know him very well — nor did he know me well — because I work in Cork. Anyway we had a fabulous time and spent most of the fortnight together. When it came to going home, he made me promise to write to him regularly and I kept my promise. But I'm ashamed to say, I didn't get as much as a postcard from him in acknowledgement. I've had a word with my best friend in my home town, who knew I was waiting to hear from him, telling me that he has had a steady girlfriend for ages and of course has gone back home to her now.

I don't really care because I don't think he seems attractive out of those glorious surroundings where we met, but I do think he has the manners of a pig. Anyway I'm back to all my friends in Dublin and I've almost forgotten what he look like. I just thought you'd like to know what kind of boys are around today.

Yours sincerely
Disillusioned

Holiday Romance Fades like a Suntan

A. I hate to burst your bubble — and I'm grateful for your kind thought of letting Granny Grunt here know 'what kind of boys are around today' — but the fact is that there never was a time when *those* sorts of boys were not around, particularly when they're far from home.

My dear girl, this is and was always known as a 'Holiday Romance', but unfortunately the experience at the time hurts. Please don't let it sour your attitude towards the entire opposite sex. My reason for using your letter is because this is the season for instant romance. I'm directing it particularly to any one of you going away on package tours at the weekend, because this day next week you might be well wondering how many guests your parents can afford to invite to the wedding. Then about a fortnight later you come home writing 'DEAR FRANKIE, I met the most fabulous boy etc, etc.'

Don't despair, enjoy yourselves and remember, the sad memories of a romantic disappointment will fade away, just like the suntan.

I'm Trendy

Dear Frankie,

I was reading your column this evening and I simply had to sit down and write to you. My case is a bit similar to the man in his early forties who had taken his 20-year-old girlfriend off on an expensive holiday and now she is treating him like dirt.

While I'm not yet in my forties, I must confess I'm over thirty and my girlfriend has just celebrated her 21st birthday. Well I've not given her lots of nice presents — not a holiday in an exotic place like the other man who wrote to you, I couldn't afford that — but things like jewellery and a handbag for instance. Anyway we do get on well together — most of the time — but she can be very offhand and I think I'm a bit too nice for her and I wonder is it because of my age difference.

I'll confess I'm actually 31 — nearly 32. She doesn't go out with anyone else except me, but there are certain areas where our tastes differ. I like classical music, she likes rock concerts. I went to one with her and I nearly went mad, but I pretended to enjoy it. On the other hand nothing would make her come to a concert with me, and I think there should be a bit of give and take. I like going to the races on a Saturday. She likes to meet her friends and listen to the buskers in town. I dress pretty trendy — not just for her — I always was interested in the current fashion for men, so we don't have a problem there. In fact now that I'm putting this in writing, I don't think we have many problems at all — it's just that I'm a bit conscious of the age gap. A few words from you might help.

Yours sincerely
Ronnie

I'm Trendy

A. Now you may be keeping up with the current fashions in men's clothes but you are a bit out of date if you are still thinking about an age gap at 31. I think your 21-year-old girlfriend has more maturity than you have, despite the ten years between you — which at your stage of life is nothing. Take the concerts for instance. She was quite right not to go to a concert that didn't interest her — and you were a fool to go to a rock concert if you don't like rock. Obviously she has plenty of friends who do like the same kind of music as she does and no doubt you're in the same position where classical music is concerned. I think you'd enjoy it much more by going alone — it's far too personal to try to share it with someone who doesn't understand it.

As for the rock concerts, you must have known that this calls for audience participation and no pretence in the world would have convinced her or anyone else that you enjoyed it. No matter how close you two may be, you're not Siamese twins, and now is the time for both of you to make it clear that you intend to pursue your own interests. Don't try and be someone you're not — your girlfriend is ten years younger and she knows this already.

As you said yourself, I don't think you have many problems at all, but remember this, there are few sights more off-putting to a woman, than the spectacle of a man making a fool of himself trying to please her. On the other hand, there are few things more annoying to a man than a woman who is too childish not to make an effort to please him. Don't worry about it. She'll catch up with you sooner than you think.

I'm No Snob

Dear Frankie,

I have what I am quite sure is an unusual problem because in the past four years, I've never missed your column and I don't recall my particular dilemma ever featuring in your correspondence. I'm not going into too many details — to start with let me tell you I've been happily married to a good man for the past seven years, and we have three lovely small children. When we first met, he had a very low paid job — a sort of messenger cum dispatch boy in a newspaper (not the *Evening Press*). Anyway, like myself he came from quite a poor family and had a limited education but was determined to better himself and I've got to admit I helped him all I could. He studied at night classes, got his Leaving Cert, then went on to more night classes at the College in Rathmines and as time went on he got one promotion after another and is now a well-paid executive in . . . I won't say where.

His work entails attending a lot of business clubs and institute meetings of which he is a member and, of course, also the social side of these groups — to which I accompany him. He's done so well that we have a nice house in a suburban estate which I love and where we have lots of good neighbours and families, all of them our friends.

I'm still very proud, but there's one drawback. In spite of all the academic learning, he's never acquired good table manners. Not only does he at times use wrong knives and forks, but when he gets animated in a conversation, I've seen him with his elbows on the table, and the knife and fork pointing to the ceiling. I cringe with embarrassment in front the executives' wives, and can't believe this isn't noticeable (his behaviour I mean). Yet he's one of the most popular and well-liked men in his group. Don't think I'm a snob

I'm No Snob

please, but I seem to get so tensed up about that and I don't want to hurt his feelings, because I think he's the most wonderful man in the world.

He's quite oblivious about his mistakes and is completely at ease in any company. I'm just worried about what they think of him and I couldn't bear him to be hurt. Should I point this out to him — to keep up with his colleagues. I've read a lot of books on etiquette.

Yours sincerely
Embarrassed

I'm No Snob

A. I don't think you're a snob . . . I just think your own sense of inferiority is rising to the surface and if you don't control it, you're seriously endangering your marriage. It's not your husband's table manners that need overhauling . . . it's your attitude and your over-concern about the opinions of 'those other wives', who for all you know are probably just as nervous as you are at those social/business gatherings. What really counts is a feeling of ease, and your husband is obviously perfectly at ease with everyone regardless of class or position. You should admire him for that, and try to emulate him. Those executives' wives are the same as any other wives . . . it's their husbands' positions which gave them the importance you're investing in them. You'll have to make your own decision in the end, but if your self-assurance depends on risking his self-confidence, where's the gain? He's doing all right as he is, maybe you should try to follow his example.

THE BEST IS YET TO COME

Stand Up and Be Counted

Dear Frankie,
I've been going with this girl for over two years now. We're both 26, we love each other very much and we want to get married. I've recently started my own business, which is going very well and I know it's going to get even better. It's one of those safe occupations — well as safe as anything in the business world today — but I've no doubts about the future and we would be very comfortably off. Let me say, we are already in a financial position to get married and have our own home, but her parents aren't mad about the idea as they think we should wait until I'm much better off.

Frankie, her parents and my parents get on very well together, in fact they are good friends and my future in-laws like me personally, but they're a bit overcareful regarding a secure future for us.

Anyway there's also a small matter of a modest legacy which will be coming to my girlfriend when she's 30 — something to do with her family's farm — but she says it's not worth waiting another four years for that. Her parents want her to wait so that we'd at least have an additional income when we marry. She wants us to go ahead now, but I'm half thinking we should wait until my business grows. What do you think? Her parents would be better pleased with me if we waited. I really do love her very much, but maybe they're right.

Yours sincerely
Anon

Stand Up and Be Counted

A. Well, your business may be growing but I'm beginning to wonder if you personally are not in danger of going through life one step forward and two steps back. Whatever happened to that air of confidence which showed through in the opening sentences of your letter? I just hope it wasn't the thought of the modest legacy which lies ahead of your patient girlfriend in four years time. Or is it perhaps the fact that you don't want to displease her parents? If you let yourself be overawed by her, you're putting yourself in a hopeless situation.

The situation seems pretty clear to me. You're an honest man with a business of your own, an ambition to build it up and a girl you love who wants to marry you. Now if she can face facts, why can't you? I don't want to be too hard on you. It is a difficult position for you, but then marriage isn't an easy matter at the best of times. However, I can't help feeling that a wife who loves you and believes in you would be a greater stimulus to success than the belief that you have to prove yourself to her parents before you take the step forward.

One thing about marriage, it separates the men from the boys and it also brings you face to face with the realities of life, which is far better than denying your own instincts in order to accept someone else's scale of values. I think your time has come to stand up and be counted — preferably at the altar rails.

Man Eater

Dear Frankie,

I'm 28, single and quite attractive — but I am very unhappy. I don't know why I behave the way I do, but I simply eat up every — well almost every — man I meet, whether it's at work, parties or just casual social gatherings. I'm just addicted to men like some people are addicted to chocolate or alcohol!

Now, I like my lifestyle and I don't see anything morally wrong in my attitude to sex, but I'm unhappy because my female colleagues at work are beginning to despise me and are making no effort to hide their contempt for me. I would try and change my job, but I work in a specialised field so it wouldn't be easy for me to do that. I'm not intruding on any man who is tied up with any of the girls I work with — yet they (the girls) are barely civil to me and never include me in any outside social events connected with the firm. What should I do about this? I'm not hurting anyone.

Yours sincerely
Feeling Outcast

Man Eater

A. You most certainly are hurting someone, yourself. How can you reconcile the fact that you are miserable and unhappy and at the same time claim that you like your lifestyle? Since most people are too busy thinking about themselves and their own problems to find time to despise anyone else — and since contempt is frequently a disguise for envy — I suspect that your female colleagues couldn't care less about your promiscuity and it's your own self-contempt you are reading into them.

If you want to become one of the girls again, I think it is essential that you discipline yourself and put a self-imposed ban on your sexual romps, during office hours for a start.

I don't think any of your colleagues are jealous of you. I'm afraid it's more a case of you boring them to death, making a bit of a laughing stock of yourself at the same time, and worst of all, giving them cause to feel sorry for you. On a more serious note, if you had written to me about food addiction for instance — an addiction which afflicts many people — I would tell you that the first thing you must find out is WHY you eat too much, and remind you that medically it has been proved that most overeaters actually hate food. You can draw your own conclusions from that bit of useful information.

I would advise you to have a chat with your doctor who will no doubt refer you to a psychologist who will get to the root cause of your sex addiction and your unhappiness.

You are worried — or you wouldn't have written to me or anyone else — but I'm glad you got your worries off your mind. The next step is medical advice.

Dear Frankie,

I've been widowed for nearly ten years and since then I have had a few hopeless affairs, the one worse than the other. I really shouldn't be complaining because I have a great family, all happily married and, in fact, I'm a grandmother. Wouldn't you think I should start behaving like one instead of getting involved in the romantic scene?

I also have a well-paid job, but needless to say, having been used to having a man in my life, I feel there's something missing. Maybe I should settle for a solitary existence and act my age. What do you think Frankie?

Yours sincerely
Doris

Rule Book for the Romantic Granny

A. I don't think — in fact I'm certain that I have never come across a rule book telling us how grandmothers should behave, so get rid of that hang-up for a start. Only the 'Fools of Fortune' have to settle for solitary existence. I'm sure Willie Birmingham could tell you heart-rending stories of what it really means to be alone in life.

Very few people choose a solitary existence — it can be yours if that's the way you want to live your life — but the majority of people who live without family or friends have reached that lonesome state through circumstances beyond their control.

But back to your 'problem'. It's clear that you're not one of those people who would chose solitude as a way of life, but it looks as if you haven't given serious thought to what you really want, now that you're eligible again. It takes time to adjust from being half a couple to being single again and although you have been widowed for ten years, it's possible you didn't give yourself sufficient time to make that adjustment, hence those disastrous affairs.

It's perfectly natural to want a man in your life again — but not just any man. I don't care if you're a great-grandmother — you're young at heart and if you stop being over anxious, I'd say you'd be snapped up. You haven't got what it takes to indulge in casual relationships, so you should think seriously of re-marrying. But whatever the future holds for you, don't lose that romantic streak. That's what keeps us all young, vital and LIVE!

Gyrate with the Best at 36!

Dear Frankie,

My problem sounds ridiculous, even to me, but you'll probably think I'm either making it up or I've had several 'over the eight', while I'm writing to you. I'm nearly 36 and I should know better, but I'm mad about this girl of 20. She's beautiful, absolutely beautiful and also a very nice girl, or so I thought until last week. A pal of mine and his wife were going off on a week's package tour to the 'Costa del Something' and suggested that I should come with them and bring the girlfriend too. So I asked her. She said 'brilliant' and I went off and bought two all-in tickets.

As a foursome we had a great time and I thought she enjoyed it until on the return journey, she started jibing about my 'efforts to keep up with the kids at the discos', as she so elegantly put it. I nearly went mad with fury — internally of course. To save my pride, I laughed along with her but my friends were furious and attacked her for her rudeness, and they reminded her of my generosity in giving her such a lovely holiday. She apologised then, but it was too late. I didn't let her see how much it hurt, but pretended all was well and when we got to Dublin airport I got a taxi and left her home. 'When will I see you again?' she says. 'I'll give you a ring', says I, knowing full well my first move when I got home would be to cross her name off my list, which I did.

Hope I did the right thing, such ingratitude and rudeness. Just thought I'd give you an example of one of today's products, Frankie. No advice needed, but if you publish this, it might save some other idiot.

Yours sincerely
Young at Heart

Gyrate with the Best at 36!

A. Everything in life is purely relative. At 36, you're well qualified to gyrate with the best of them, either in the 'Costa del Something' or any of your own multi-discolands back here in Dublin, as well as right through most of the countryside. In a twisted way, I don't believe for a moment this girl was deliberately trying to hurt you. The excitement of the holiday was still with the four of you and no doubt you were 'flying' a bit on the journey home, all of you trying to get the last ounce out of your fortnight's break and verbally re-living the fun and the freedom you had left behind. Yes, it was hurtful and rude if you like, but not premeditated, just an unfortunate choice of banter.

Somehow or other, I always felt that behind gratitude lies resentment. 'Take back your watch, your ring, your pendant or whatever.' It's the cry that goes up as soon as a row breaks out— I'd nearly go as far as saying that serious quarrels are almost impossible until presents have changed hands. It takes exquisite tact to give a present without unknowingly sowing the seeds of a future row, but that doesn't apply in your case. The holiday is gone, you all enjoyed it, so forget that incident and think of the good times. If you don't contact her, you can be sure, she'll be on to you. Don't be too tough, she's inexperienced and immature and she hasn't yet learned that there are few things more annoying to a man, than a woman — of any age — who is too childish not to try to please him.

Was I a Little Hasty?

Dear Frankie,
    I have had the same boyfriend for the past year and a half. I've been mad about him since first we met and he's very much in love with me too. I was almost 16 when we started going together and he's a year older. Well, recently after eighteen months of a close and fantastic relationship and friendship, I felt I was ready to have sex properly for the first time in my life and I enjoyed it a lot and have no regrets. However, I can't help asking myself if I was a little hasty. Should I have waited longer, until I was older, or do most girls of today have sex at about this age?

    Although nothing has changed between us, somehow or other I feel a bit confused and am writing to ask your views. We're very happy together.

Yours sincerely
ANON

Was I a Little Hasty?

A. Methinks thou dost protest too much. In other words, you do have regrets, if you're looking back on what you did with worry and a trace of sorrow. Should you have waited longer? It doesn't matter now — you didn't wait longer. Do most girls of today have sex at about your age? Maybe, perhaps some do and some don't, but that doesn't matter either.

Surely when considering the most intimate decisions of your life, you're not going to be concerned whether it's fashionable or not? One thing I can tell you for sure, you're certainly not the first girl of 17 or $17^1/_2$ to have 'sex properly', as you term it, and I'm sure you won't be the last.

Stop looking back because it merely prevents you from looking ahead. Your status among women has changed subtly and you must enter your new condition with intelligence and a sense of responsibility. Having made love with your boyfriend once, you will probably continue to do so, but are you going to stay with him exclusively?

You must now consider relationships with the opposite sex in a way that goes deeper than just having fun. It would be most regrettable if you ceased to be an independent, learning, achieving human being. Be happy — and be careful.

Life Begins at Forty

D*ear Frankie,*

I am a widow in my fifties — actually I'm nearer 50 than 60 — and for the past three years I have been very friendly with a man in his early forties. Now we know we're in love and he wants us to get married. He had a brief marriage when he was very young — but he's free legally to get married again, so there's no obstacle. I am the one putting forward the obstacles. I tell him he will be depriving himself of family life, but he insists that he never was interested in having children, and although I keep pointing out that he should find a young person to marry, he says if I don't marry him, he'll stay single.

I certainly don't want to lose his friendship, but wouldn't it be unfair of me to accept him? You see, I'm sure to go first and I wouldn't want him to have a life of loneliness after I'm gone. At my age I should know what to do, but I don't and I'd like your opinion on my situation. I find it very difficult to resist his pleading because I really do love him.

Yours sincerely
Mixed-up and Muddled

Life Begins at Forty

A. You're not the only one mixed-up and muddled. I've spent quite a considerable time trying to make out the age gap between you and your persistent suitor and I might as well be back in school grappling with those incredible maths problems which always seemed to end up telling us 'the answer is in apples'. Anyway with the help of the pocket calculator, I deduce that you are maybe nine or ten years older than this man— so what's your problem?

Recently I was reading an article on the current Hollywood and world sex symbols of the female variety, starting with Liz Taylor (she of the eight marriages and seven husbands). This lovely list included Joan Collins — then 49 and holding — Linda 'Sue Ellen' Gray, Racquel Welch, Victoria Principal, Linda Evans and of course Jackie Kennedy Onassis. The feature was headed 'Life begins at Forty . . . and at Fifty' — so if I were you I'd first of all rid myself of this age complex which seems to be the only factor in preventing you from marrying this man.

You've obviously put this argument to him and he's trying to see sense, but if you persist long enough in pleading your case against marriage 'for his sake', there's a danger that you might score your point — but lose the man. And tell me, what makes you so sure you'll go first just because he's a bit younger than you? Sadly death is the great equaliser and the number of years we've been here have very little to do with our destiny. Illness or accident can strike anytime, so don't dwell on that aspect of your situation. If you're over 50 then the law of averages makes it more likely that you have more years behind than you have ahead of you — all the more reason to make the rest of your life as full as possible.

In other words, don't just sit there, do something. You could start by drawing up a list of guests and then making a booking for the wedding reception.

Mummy's Boy

Dear Frankie,

I'm in my late twenties and getting married shortly to a very nice man of my own age. The trouble is that we will be living with his mother when we marry and she is still terribly possessive about him and still treats him like a child . . . she even chooses his clothes for him and tells him what he should or should not wear.

There are eight in his family (his father died some years ago) and all his brothers and sisters are married and live quite a distance away. They were all brought up in this family house and farm. My fiancé was the only one who showed interest in the farm so that's why we're stuck to move in with his mother. He keeps telling me not to mind her, that she's really easy to get on with. But she's constantly at me about what he likes and dislikes and not to keep him up too late at night because he's to get up early in the morning and things like that. Another thing is, she has never once referred to our forthcoming marriage in any conversations — and the other thing that bothers me is that she's quite a dowdy woman, never makes an effort to smarten herself up. So I'm dreading asking my friends to the house when we're married. My family are quite different— in fact they're all (particularly my parents) very independent. Could you please tell me how to deal with her when we're married?

Don't misunderstand me, Frankie, she's a nice woman and seems to like me. It's her attitude to her son that I object to. In fact I quite like her myself.

Yours sincerely
Anon

Mummy's Boy

A. Well, you could have fooled me. You weren't exactly giving her a glowing reference in the bulk of your letter — in fact I was in the deepest depths of depression at the thought of what lay before you until I got to the last bit. So, she likes you and you like her, but you don't like her attitude to your future husband . . . and you ask me how you will deal with her when you're married.

It seems to me that you need to clean the air before you marry. It will be too late to tackle the problem after you become Mrs. X and move into your new home. Now is the time to discuss it with her. It's up to you to enlist your boyfriend's support and then sit down to a family conference. Remember, a family conference, not a family row. If this house comfortably accommodated eight children and their parents, there must be plenty of space for you to map out a plan by which you two newly-weds and your mother-in-law can all live together but separate — if you follow me.

Don't forget, she will need her privacy too, so don't just go on making the wedding arrangements without knowing exactly what you're letting yourself into. Start off with some friendly overtures. For all you know, she may be scared stiff of the thought of your arrival. As she seems to be a quiet, motherly woman it's up to you to be assertive — but not too aggressive — about this. Neither of you needs to submit to the other, if you go about it the right way — in fact your own parents might be a help here because from what you've told me, right now you all seem to be a collection of strangers.

I'm afraid you've been so obsessed with your domestic problems, I'm wondering have you any idea of the pressures involved in farming today or the number of working hours he has to put in to his work to make it pay. Think about that.

I Know I Will Make the Perfect Husband

Dear Frankie,
I am 35 and an executive with an electronic company in Dublin. I don't smoke, rarely drink, and I'm considered quite a good-looking chap. I've been trying very hard to meet a girl who could meet my standards and whom I would ultimately marry, but so far I have failed.

I consider myself an ordinary person, humble, compassionate and understanding and I am determined to marry a sincere Irish girl, but I don't think lovers of the bright lights would be suitable as I am from a small town myself and I like the simple life.

I have been out with hundreds of girls, but the majority of them seem only interested in a good time — on a one-night-only basis. That's not for me because now I'm ready for marriage.

Where are all those innumerable girls in their mid-twenties who write to you enquiring about prospective husbands? I can't understand the complaints I hear about Irish bachelors and their reluctance to marry. There's nothing more I wish than to marry and settle down with a nice sensible settled wife. I know that I will make a perfect husband.

Yours sincerely
Donny

I Know I Will Make the Perfect Husband

A. First of all, I would suggest you try to rid yourself of this inferiority complex and lack of self-confidence. Secondly, I think you're mixing me up with someone else. I have no recollection of letters from innumerable girls in their mid-twenties enquiring about prospective husbands — but that's a minor matter.

However now that I have you, even though chance has brought us together, I trust you won't be offended if I make a few comments on your sad situation.

This may come as a shock but women are actually human beings and very few of us, if any, would be particularly pleased to find ourselves scrutinised like items in a Christmas catalogue in your search for the most trouble-free model of the current trend in nice settled wives.

I've never known a woman who thinks of herself like that, however sensible and settled she may be. Coming from a man who had done his share of rambling and roving, there is something offensively patronising in the very idea.

A professional housekeeper might not object — if the salary and home comforts were acceptable — but I suspect that the man who says he's looking for a nice, settled, sensible wife means that he's really searching for an unpaid housekeeper with a civil tongue in her head. I'm afraid women are more demanding and difficult to please nowadays than they used to be.

Romance without Romantic Explosion

Dear Frankie,

My story may be a little old-fashioned for your column, but I thought you'd like to hear about it. This year I celebrate my seventy-eighth birthday and my wife celebrates her seventy-sixth.

When I was 15, a new family moved in next door — the family included 13-year-old twin sisters. We all grew up together, went to the same schools and when we left school some years later, I knew I really loved one of the twins very much.

When I told her of my feelings, I found she felt the same and eventually we got engaged, to the great delight of both families. Then tragedy struck — my fiancée was killed in an accident and my world was shattered. I went off to the States, stayed there for three years and then came home. I was delighted to find the family next door still there, and my late fiancée's twin sister was still living at home and was unmarried.

Naturally, we renewed our friendship and went for long walks together, but we never talked of the past. We found ourselves content with each other's company, renewing and sharing an old friendship. I knew she was fond of me and of course I was very fond of her with great affection. Finally I suggested marriage on the basis of our friendship and affection — and so we got married.

We had four lovely children — all married now with families of their own. In fact we have eight grandchildren and four great-grandchildren! They all live within ten to twenty miles of us and today we are one big happy family. Our marriage was based on love, affection, respect and friendship and although I have never forgotten my first love, I look back on a wonderful life of happiness with my wife, even though you may find it hard to believe that this could happen with a couple who were never madly 'in love' with each other. Can you as a woman understand that?

Yours sincerely
Contented

Romance without Romantic Explosion

A. I most certainly understand it very well and allowing for the remarkable circumstances surrounding your story, what happened to you and your wife confirms what I have often written to correspondents on this page. Not that romance and being wildly in love are to be discounted — indeed your story is highly romantic — but that romance by itself is a dangerous basis for marriage and that affection, respect and friendship are essential elements in an enduring marriage.

It seems to me that a lifetime of contentment is not to be despised simply because it didn't start out with a 'romantic explosion', and I have no doubt that a great number of our readers will be moved by your story.